THE IRISH QUOTATION BOOK

Happy
71 st (Claudia

(same as myself)

April 16, 1994

As ever,
Marie

The Irish
Quotation Book

A Literary Companion

Edited by

MAINCHÍN SEOIGHE

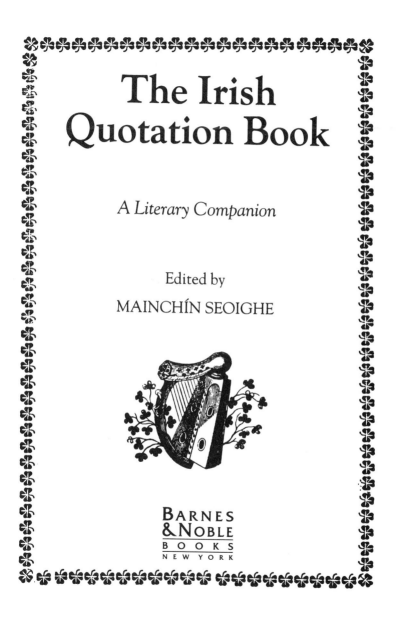

BARNES
&NOBLE
BOOKS
NEW YORK

This edition published by Barnes & Noble, Inc.,
by arrangement with Robert Hale, Inc.

1993 Barnes & Noble Books

ISBN 1-56619-235-8

Printed and bound in the United States of America

M 9 8 7 6 5 4 3 2 1

Preface

ecause there was such a wealth of material to choose from, selecting quotations for this book was no easy task. Obviously, writers such as Swift, Goldsmith, Moore, Mangan, Wilde, Synge, Shaw, Yeats, Joyce, O'Casey, O'Connor and O'Faoláin would figure in it; so, too, would well known writers of more recent times; as well as poetic officials and observant travellers like Edmund Spenser, Arthur Young, the Halls and H.V. Morton, who wrote perceptively of what they saw while they sojourned in Ireland. Then there were the very many lesser known writers, and examples of the work of some of these had to be included if the book was to be truly representative of Ireland and of Irish writing.

Nor was that all. Ireland was a country of two languages, with Irish the predominant literary medium up to the mid seventeenth century. English however gradually began to come to the fore from the beginning of the eighteenth century, even though Irish was still to remain the spoken language of nearly half the population up to the early decades of the nineteenth century. Today, English is the predominant literary medium, though Irish, as a literary medium, still continues to contribute to the age-old Gaelic literary tradition.

And so I have included a certain number of quotations in Irish, with their English translations, in the book; where not otherwise stated these are by me. In the case of Old Irish quotations, which range from the seventh to the twelfth century, only the translations are given. A Glossary and Notes appear at the end of the book.

I thought it best to arrange the quotations by theme, in so far as it was possible to do so, without, however, introducing specific section headings. The reader will therefore find, for example, a run of quotations dealing with Irish places, another with Irish people, another with Irish humour, another with Irish spirituality, another with Irish love songs, and so on.

In all, excerpts from more than 120 writers, spanning a period of some 1,300 years, have been brought together in this anthology of quotations which, I hope, will give the reader a genuine taste of Ireland.

MAINCHÍN SEOIGHE

Acknowledgements

My thanks to the following who helped me track down elusive quotations, lent books, or otherwise helped while I was compiling this book: Damien Brady, County Librarian, and staff of County Library, Limerick; Eileen Mac Mahon, acting City Librarian, and staff of Limerick City Library; Dr Gerard Lyne, National Library of Ireland, Dublin; Ruairí Brugha, Dublin; Déaglán de Bréadún, Dublin; Maureen Lonergan, M.A., Cork; Christine Hedderman, Bruree; Máirín Uí Loinsigh, Kilmallock; Luaí Ó Murchú, Listowel; Gabriel Fitzmaurice, Moyvane; Antony Farrell, Dublin; Alice Taylor, Innishannon; Bernadette Smyth, Newbridge; Donogh and John O'Brien, Dublin; Síle de Cléir, Limerick; Liam Ó Duibhir, Clonmel.

My thanks too to the following for permission to include copyright material in the book: Methuen & Co for excerpts from *In Search of Ireland* by H.V. Morton; Hutchinson & Co for excerpt from *Brendan Behan's Island* by Brendan Behan; A.P. Watt Ltd, for excerpts from *Here's Ireland* by

Acknowledgements

Bryan Mac Mahon; Hamlyn Publishing Group Ltd, for excerpt from *Celtic Mythology* by Proinsias Mac Cana; Oxford University Press for excerpts from *The Western Island* and *The Irish Tradition*, both by Robin Flower; The Lilliput Press for excerpt from *Ulster: The Common Ground* by E. Estyn Evans, and two excerpts from *Escape from the Anthill*, by Hubert Butler; Dr Peter Kavanagh and The Goldsmith Press for 'Gut your Man' and quatrain from 'A Christmas Childhood,' both by Patrick Kavanagh; Gill & Macmillan for translations from *The Love Songs of Connacht* by Douglas Hyde, and for excerpts from *The Hidden Ireland* by Daniel Corkery, and from *The Black North* by Aodh de Blácam; Irish Academic Press for excerpt from *The Surnames of Ireland* by Edward MacLysaght; Education Co. of Ireland for excerpt from *Songs of the Irish*, by Donal O'Sullivan; Brandon Book Publishers for excerpts from *To School through the Fields* by Alice Taylor; Macmillan Ltd for excerpt from *Irish Miles* by Frank O'Connor, and for excerpts from poems by James Stephens; David Higham Associates for excerpts from *My Ireland* by Kate O'Brien; the Purcell Family for excerpt from *The GAA in its Time* by Pádraig Puirséal; Donnchadh O'Corráin and Fidelma Maguire for extract from their book *Gaelic Personal Names*; Benedict Kiely for excerpt from *Poor Scholar* and *Capuchin Annual* 1945/6; The Blackstaff Press for poem 'The Irish Dimension', by John Hewitt; Mrs Evelyn O'Nolan for excerpt from 'Cruiseckeen Lawn' (from *Irish Times*), by her late husband Brian O'Nolan (pseudonyms, Flann O'Brien and Myles na Gopaleen); The British Academy for excerpts from lecture on 'The Gaelic Storyteller' by J.H. Delargy; C.J. Fallon Publishers for quotations from Luke Gernon, Dr Massari and Le Sieur de la Boullaye le Gouz, in *Ireland – From the Flight of the Earls to Grattan's Parliament*.

I would again like to thank the publishers, authors and

Acknowledgements

other holders of copyright material who kindly gave permission to include excerpts from it in this book. I made every effort to trace all such copyright holders, and apologize if any have been inadvertently overlooked.

M.S.

She is a rich and rare land;
Oh! she's a fresh and fair land;
She is a dear and rare land –
This native land of mine.
THOMAS DAVIS
Ireland – My Land

... the real beauty of Ireland is much more than skin-deep.
And it can hide itself. And I truly think that Ireland at its
best is still a secret for connoisseurs.
KATE O'BRIEN
My Ireland, 1962

I ... sent for Mr Butler, who was now all full of his high
discourse in praise of Ireland ... but so many lies I never
heard in praise of anything as he told of Ireland.
SAMUEL PEPYS
Diary, 28 July 1660

Acutely conscious though we all are of the misery and desolation in which the greater part of the world is plunged, let us turn aside for a moment to that ideal Ireland that we would have. That Ireland which we dreamed of would be the home of a people who valued material wealth only as the basis of right living, of a people who were satisfied with frugal comfort and devoted their leisure to the things of the spirit – a land whose countryside would be bright with cosy homesteads, whose fields and villages would be joyous with the sounds of industry, with the romping of sturdy children, the contests of athletic youths and the laughter of comely maidens, whose firesides would be forums for the wisdom of serene old age. It would, in a word, be the home of a people living the life that God desires that man should live.

ÉAMON DE VALERA
in a broadcast as Taoiseach (Head of Government) to
the nation, St Patrick's Day, 1943

The language in which these aims were expressed was the language of that era – 'frugal comfort,' 'comely maidens' – and may have a dated and stilted sound to our ears today, but the essential point is that we can still understand and be inspired by the ideals and concepts behind the language.

ALBERT REYNOLDS[1]
addressing a meeting 28 December 1991 – see
previous quotation

The noblest share of earth is the far western world
Whose name is written Scottia[2] in the ancient books;
Rich in goods, in silver, jewels, cloth and gold,
Benign to the body in air and mellow soil.

With honey and with milk flow Ireland's lovely plains,
With silk and arms, abundant fruit, with art and men.
    LIAM DE PAOR
    from the Latin of Donatus, 9th century bishop of
    Fiesole, in *Monumenta Germaniae historica, Poet. Lat.
    aevi Carol.* Reprinted in 'The Age of the Viking
    Wars' in *The Course of Irish History*, ed. T.W. Moody
    & F.X. Martin, 1967

So I have come into Wicklow, where the fields are sharply
green, where a wild beauty hides in the glens, where sudden
surprising vistas open up as the road rises and falls; and here
I smell for the first time the incense of Ireland, the smoke of
turf fires, and here for the first time I see the face of the Irish
countryside.
    H.V. MORTON
    In Search of Ireland, 1930

I will arise and go now, and go to Innisfree,
And a small cabin build there of clay and wattles made:
Nine bean rows will I have there, a hive for the honey
bee,
And live alone in the bee-loud glade
    W.B. YEATS
    'The Lake Isle of Innisfree'

Oh, Limerick is beautiful
As everybody knows,
And by that city of my heart
How proud old Shannon flows.
    MICHAEL SCANLAN (1833–1917)

The Shannon is a formidable water; nothing parochial
about it, nothing of prattle or girlish dream. It sweeps in

13

and out of the ocean and the world according to the rules of far-out-tides, and in association with dangerous distances. So its harbour has been long accustomed to news and trouble in and out, and in the general movement of time Limerick has been shaped as much by invasions and sieges as by acts of God and the usual weatherings. It is for Ireland therefore a representative city: whatever happened to Ireland happened also here – and some things happened to Ireland because of things that happened here.

> KATE O'BRIEN
> *My Ireland*, 1962

Limerick was,
Dublin is,
And Cork will be
The finest city of the three.
> OLD SAYING

Sweet Auburn[3]! lovliest village of the plain,
Where health and plenty cheer'd the labouring swain,
Where smiling Spring its earliest visit paid,
And parting Summer's lingering blooms delay'd:
Dear lovely bowers of innocence and ease,
Seats of my youth, when every sport could please:
How often have I loiter'd o'er thy green,
Where humble happiness endear'd each scene!
How often have I paused on every charm,
The shelter'd cot, the cultivated farm,
The never-failing brook, the busy mill,
The decent church that topp'd the neighbouring hill.
> OLIVER GOLDSMITH
> *The Deserted Village*

14

... no place has given me a clearer picture of early Christianity than the strange little ruined city of Glendalough,[4] in Co. Wicklow. I do not think Ireland can have anything more lovely to show than this heavenly little valley, with its two small lakes lying cupped in a hollow of the hills ... A tall, round tower rises above the trees at the lakeside, one of those towers peculiar to Ireland, and built nearly 1,000 years ago as a belfry and a refuge from the Danes.

H.V. MORTON
In Search of Ireland, 1930

The counties of Cork and Kerry are my favourites of all. They are unbelievably beautiful. Going from Glengariff when I caught my first sight of the Lakes of Killarney, with their natural bulwark of mountains, I stopped in breath-taking wonder and found myself saying, 'My God, how lovely!'

JOHN CYRIL MAUDE, MP
in Irish Press, 14 September 1951

Every graciousness and softness that nature has denied the mountains have been poured out into the rich valley of Killarney. It is almost too good to be true; almost too opulent to be quite credible. You feel, as you look down on it, that it might at any moment dissolve into mist, leaving you in the stern reality of the hills ...
> H.V. MORTON
> *In Search of Ireland*, 1930

In autumn the red and brown of the mountains and trees colour the cooling air. You can leave Killarney behind you, walk along the road with the grey wall that hides the beauties of Muckross on your right hand, and the moving shoulder of Torc above you on the left, up and up until everything touristed and ticketed is below in the deep valley, until you feel the colour of the mountains, soaking into your eyes, your hair, the fragile fabric of skin, until the silence of the high places has seeped into your soul.
> BENEDICT KIELY
> 'Land without Stars', in *Capuchin Annual*, 1945/6

By Killarney's lakes and fells, emerald isle and winding bays,
Mountain paths and woodland dells, memory every fondly strays.
Bounteous nature loves all lands, beauty wanders everywhere,
Footprints leave on many strands, but her home is surely there.
Angels fold their wings and rest in that Eden of the West,
Beauty's home Killarney, heaven's reflex Killarney.
> JULIUS BENEDICT
> from the opera *The Lily of Killarney*, 1862

Then came Cashel! ... 'the great vision of the guarded mount' stood directly poised on the chimney-pots of the gay painted street. Below everything was Georgian; shadowed, solid, decorous and domestic to the last degree, and above, each outline from the lifted finger-tip of the belfry to the toy towers of Cormac's Chapel was remote, romantic and insubstantial ...

It was all grey, the cathedral with its angle tower, the belfry with its conical top, even the steep flagged roof of Cormac's Chapel was remote; a pure, pearly, translucent grey which seemed to float and melt into the evening sky, as though it were in another dimension; an Irish Olympus.

    FRANK O'CONNOR
    Irish Miles, 1947

And I wouldn't care much for Sierra Leone,
If I hadn't seen Killenaule,
And the man that was never in Mullinahone
Shouldn' say he had travelled at all!

    CHARLES J. BOLAND
    Rare Clonmel, ed. James Maher

Oh, sweet Adare! oh, lovely vale!
Oh, soft retreat of sylvan splendour!
Nor summer sun, nor morning gale
E'er hailed a scene more softly tender.

    GERALD GRIFFIN

Kilmallock must be a place of high antiquity ... It ... preserves a greater share of magnificence, even in its ruins, than anything I have yet seen in Ireland. I call it the Irish Balbec.

    DR CAMPBELL
    Philosophical Survey of the South of Ireland, 1775

There is something inexpressibly weird about those millions of mathematically formed pillars which thrust themselves upward at the edge of the sea. And the whole scene is a shade of metallic grey. I have never seen stones that so closely resemble iron or steel. The (Giant's) Causeway has a queerly modern look! It is Cubist.

> H.V. MORTON
> *In Search of Ireland*, 1930

There is a stone that whoever kisses
Oh, he never misses to grow eloquent,
Tis he may clamber to a lady's chamber,
Or become a Member of Parliament:
A clever spouter he'll soon turn out, or
An out-and-outer to be let alone;
Don't hope to hinder him, or to bewilder him,
Sure he's a pilgrim from the Blarney Stone.

> FRANCIS SYLVESTER MAHONY ('FR. PROUT')
> 'The Blarney Stone'

He who kissed the Blarney Stone is assumed to be endowed with a fluent and persuasive tongue, although it may be associated with insincerity, the term 'blarney' generally being used to characterise words that are meant neither to be 'honest nor true'.

> MR & MRS S.C. HALL
> *Hall's Ireland*, 1841

Out from Dunquin Pier I go with Dr Maurice Harmon, that rare judge of literature, his wife and children: we were Blasket-bound in a black-backed canvas currach. The Blaskets were hidden in a fog. Presently, Dunquin, Ireland, Europe fell away and we rode as ghosts on ghostly water. Orange nylon lines and hooks garishly feathered brought in

The Blarney Stone

mackerel to thump the ribs of our frail vessel ... later we rode into a ghostly cove under the cliffs of the deserted Great Blasket. Up the lichened pathway we moved ... Wreaths of fog swirled about us ...

    BRYAN MAC MAHON
    Here's Ireland, 1971

Tá Connacht molta dá mbeinn im thost,
Connacht aoibhinn gan aon locht.
    ANON, 17th century

Translation:
    Connacht were praised though I said naught,
    Lovely Connacht without a fault.

Kilkenny values itself upon its superior gentility and urbanity. It is much frequented by the neighbouring gentry as a country residence, has a stand of nine sedan chairs and is not without the appearance of an agreeable place.

    DR CAMPBELL
    Philosophical Survey of the South of Ireland, 1775

Dublin city, with its bay and pleasant villas – city of bellowing slaves – villas of genteel dastards – lies now behind us, and the sun has set behind the blue peaks of Wicklow, as we steam past Bray Head, where the Vale of Shanganagh, sloping softly from the Golden Spears, sends its bright river murmuring to the sea. And I am on the first stage of my way, faring to what regions of unknown horror? And may never, never, – never more, O Ireland, – my mother and my Queen! – see vale, or hill, or murmuring stream of thine.

    JOHN MITCHEL
    Jail Journal – part of his entry for 27 May 1848

The Forces of the Irish Republic, which was proclaimed in Dublin, on Easter Monday, 24th April, have been in possession of the central part of the capital since 12 noon on that day ... If they do not win this fight, they will at least have deserved to win it ... Already they have won a great thing. They have redeemed Dublin from many shames, and made her name splendid among the names of cities.

    P.H. PEARSE
    statement issued from headquarters of Easter Rising,
    28 April 1916

Dublin in the early morning with the sun shining, is a city the colour of claret. The red-brick Georgian mansions, with fine doors, fanlights, and little iron balconies at the first-floor windows, stand back in well-bred reticence against wide roads, quiet and dignified, as if the family had just left by stage-coach. Dublin shares with Edinburgh the air of having been a great capital.

    H.V. MORTON
    In Search of Ireland, 1930

The Leinsterman laughs:
Seek him out for an evening's delight, –
And the Connachtman, too,
For his songs and the tales that he tells:
The Ulsterman, – he
Is your need when it comes to a fight:
But the Munsterman: he
Both in word and in deed excels!

    AODH DE BLÁCAM
    translation of anonymous 17th century Irish poem
    made in 1942 for the compiler of this book

The whole of South Connemara, shelving out from the hills to the sea, is silvery, level, water-striped and overflowing with light; in subtlety and delicacy its folding lands are as unlike the dramatic passes and valleys of the northern region as its guardian Bens are different from Maam Turk ... there is often an illusion that all is afloat, an uncertainty between hill and sky, an interchange of water and stone which the indescribably clear light seems paradoxically to exaggerate.

> KATE O'BRIEN
> *My Ireland*, 1962

On the morrow I had arranged to go to the Aran Islands. I reached the quay as the boat was casting off, its passengers animated by a spirit of adventurous gaiety ... There was a Federal Judge from Kansas and his lawyer friend, two priests, an American film-maker and a group of courteous but shy islanders talking together in Irish ... After a few hours chugging the islands came into view and presently we saw the crowds gathered on Kilronan Quay on Innismore ... As the gangway clattered down I clucked to a jarvey, thus engaging a side-car for our excursion ... the sun shone brilliantly ...

> BRYAN MAC MAHON
> *Here's Ireland*, 1971

> Under bare Ben Bulben's head
> In Drumcliff churchyard Yeats is laid.
> And ancestor was rector there
> Long years ago, a church stands near,
> By the road an ancient cross.
>> W.B. YEATS
>> 'Under Ben Bulben'

Ireland without her people is nothing to me.
JAMES CONNOLLY
Workers Republic, 7 July 1900

The man of Ireland is of a strong constitution, tall and big-limbed, but seldom fat, patient of heat and cold, but impatient of labour. Of nature he is prompt and ingenious, but servile, crafty and inquisitive after news, the symptoms of a conquered nation. Their speech has been accused to be a whining language, but that is among the beggars. I take it to be a smooth language well comixt of vowels and consonants and hath a pleasing cadence.
JUSTICE LUKE GERNON
from his *Discourse* in Stowe Papers, 1620

The [Irish] men are fine-looking and of incredible strength, swift runners, and ready to bear any kind of hardship with cheerfulness. They are all trained in arms, especially now that they are at war. Those who apply themselves to letters are very learned, and well fitted to the professions and sciences.

> DR MASSARI
> translated from Italian of Massari's *Diary*. Massari came to Ireland in 1645, as secretary to the Papal Nuncio

The women of Ireland are very comely creatures, tall, slender and upright. Of complexion very fayre (but freckled) with tresses of bright yellow hayre, which they chain up in curious knots and devises.

> JUSTICE LUKE GERNON
> *Discourse* in Stowe Papers, 1620

The [Irish] women are distinguished by their grace and beauty, and they are as modest as they are lovely. Their manners are marked by extreme simplicity, and they mix freely in conversation on all occasions without suspicion or jealousy. Their dress differs from ours, and is somewhat like the French. They also wear cloaks reaching to their heels and tufted locks of hair, and they go without any head-dress, content with linen bands bound up in Greek fashion, which display their natural beauty to much advantage.

> DR MASSARI
> *Diary*

The Irish are fond of strangers, and it costs little to travel among them. When a traveller of good address enters their houses with assurance, he has but to draw a box of snuff, and offer it to them; then these people receive him with

24

admiration, and give him the best they have to eat. They love the Spaniards as their brothers, the French as their friends, the Italians as their allies ...

LE SIEUR DE LA BOULLAYE LE GOUZ
translated from his *Les Voyages et Observations*, Paris, 1653

Providence has balanced very lightly this airy Irish nature. It swings to a touch. Where heavier natures creep slowly up and down according to the weight or pressure of circumstances, the Celtic temperament leaps to the weight of a feather; and you have sullen depression, or irresponsible gaiety, murderous disloyalty or more than feudal fealty, in swift and sudden alterations.

CANON P.A. SHEEHAN
Glenanaar, 1905

Another point of importance is their children not being burthensome. In all the enquiries I made into the state of the poor, I found their happiness and ease generally relative to the number of their children, and nothing considered as such a misfortune as having none.

ARTHUR YOUNG
A Tour in Ireland (1776–79), Vol. 11

It was altogether a very jolly life that I led in Ireland. I was always moving about. The Irish people did not murder me, nor did they break my head. I soon found them to be good-humoured, clever – the working class much more intelligent than those in England – economical and hospitable.

ANTHONY TROLLOPE
from his *Autobiography*

The circumstances which struck me most about the common Irish were vivacity and a great and eloquent volubility of speech; one would think they could take snuff and talk without tiring till doosmday. They are infinitely more cheerful and lively than anything we commonly see in England, having nothing of that incivility of sullen silence, with which so many enlightened Englishmen seem to wrap themselves up as if retiring within their own importance.

    ARTHUR YOUNG
    Tour in Ireland (1776–79), Vol. 11

The State recognises the Family as the natural primary and fundamental unit group of Society, and as a moral institution possessing inalienable and imprescriptible rights, antecedent and superior to all positive law. The State, therefore, guarantees to protect the Family in its constitution and authority, as the necessary basis of social order and as indispensable to the welfare of the Nation and the State.

    CONSTITUTION OF IRELAND
    from Article 41

With seven children in the family, we were reared free as birds, growing up in a world of simplicity untouched by outside influences. Our farm was our world and nature as an educator gave free rein to our imaginations; unconsciously we absorbed the natural order of things and observed the facts of life daily before our eyes. We were free to be children and to grow up at our own pace in a quiet place close to the earth.

    ALICE TAYLOR
    To School through the Fields, 1988

The white road twists like a snake between the grey walls, and over it walk strong, barelegged girls, wearing scarlet skirts and Titian-blue aprons. They swing from the hips as they walk with the grace of those who have never known shoe leather, and they carry on their backs great loads of brown seaweed in wicker baskets. Or they ride, sitting

sideways with their legs to the road, above the tails of placid donkeys, over whose backs are slung baskets piled with peat. If you speak to them they shake their tangled heads, and say something, which sounds pretty, in Irish ... Connemara.

    H.V. MORTON
    In Search of Ireland, 1930

The great Gaels of Ireland
Are the men that God made mad,
For all their wars are merry,
And all their songs are sad.
G.K. CHESTERTON

Their [the Irish] love of society is as remarkable as their curiosity is insatiable; and their hospitality to all comers, be their own poverty ever so pinching, has too much merit to be forgotten. Pleased to enjoyment with a joke, or witty repartee, they will repeat it with such expression, that the laugh will be universal.
ARTHUR YOUNG
Tour in Ireland

An Irish Row

The Irish are a fair people; – they never speak well of one another.

SAMUEL JOHNSON
letter to Dr Barnard in Boswell's *Life of Johnson*, 1775

Hard drinkers and quarrelsome, great liars, but civil, submissive and obedient.

ARTHUR YOUNG
on Irish traits in his *Tour in Ireland* (1776–79), Vol. 11

To the city of Cork belongs the honour of forwarding and establishing one of the most extraordinary moral revolutions which the history of the world records: the Temperance Movement, at the head of which is the Very Rev. Theobald Mathew, a Capuchin friar.

For centuries past, drunkenness was the shame and bane of Ireland; an Irishman, without reference to his rank in society, from the highest to the lowest, had become proverbial for intoxication, and to picture an Irishman truly, either in words or on canvas, or to represent him accurately on the stage, it was considered indispensable that he should be drunk.

MR & MRS S.C. HALL
Hall's Ireland, 1841

Not far off, at Aghaderg, is the home of the Rev. Patrick Brontë, rightly Prunty, who in England took the name Brontë after Nelson. In the sombre genius of his three remarkable daughters were the racial memories of the Ulster Gael; for the Pruntys originally came from Fermanagh where the name was A' *Phronntaigh*, meaning So-and-so 'of the Refectory' – some servant of the friars.

AODH DE BLÁCAM
The Black North, 1938

But a sudden feeling comes upon you of a new presence in the room. You look up and see, leaning against the wall almost with the air of a being magically materialized out of nothing, a slight but confident figure. The face takes your attention at once and holds it. This face is dark and thin, and there look out of it two quick and living eyes, the vivid witnesses of a fine and self-sufficing intelligence. He comes towards you, and with a grave and courteous intonation, and a picked and running phrase, bids you welcome. You have indeed come home, for this is Tomás Ó Crithin, the Island poet and story-teller.

    ROBIN FLOWER
    The Western Island, 1944

For Big Peg – Peig Mhór – is one of the finest speakers on the Island; she has so clean and finished a style of speech that you can follow all the nicest articulations of the language on her lips without any effort; she is a natural orator, with so keen a sense of the turn of phrase and the lifting rhythm appropriate to Irish that her words could be written down as they leave her lips, and they would have the effect of literature with no savour of the artificiality of composition. She is wont to illustrate her talk with tales, long and short, which come in naturally along the flow of conversation, and lighten up all our discourse of the present with the wit and wisdom and folly and vivid incident of the past.

    ROBIN FLOWER
    The Western Island, 1944

The voice of the Irish gentleman, Spanish grandee, was a welcome relief from the chorus of retaliatory rancour and self-righteousness then deafening us ... Eamon de Valera

comes out of it as a champion of the Christian chivalry we
are all pretending to admire.

> BERNARD SHAW
> commenting on Éamon de Valera's reply to Winston
> Churchill who, at the end of the Second World War,
> criticized Ireland's neutrality during the war

The clear true eyes of this man almost alone in his day
visioned Ireland as we of today would surely have her; not
free merely but Gaelic as well; not Gaelic merely but free as
well.

> P.H. PEARSE
> oration at grave of O'Donovan Rossa, 1 August 1915

Christ with me, Christ before me, Christ behind me,
Christ in me, Christ beneath me, Christ above me,
Christ on my right, Christ on my left,
Christ when I lie down, Christ when I sit down,
   Christ when I arise.
Christ in the heart of every man who thinks of me,
Christ in the mouth of every one who speaks of me,
Christ in every eye that sees me,
Christ in every ear that hears me.

> ANON.
> From *Lúireach Phádraig* (St Patrick's Breastplate). 8th
> c. Translated from the Irish by Kuno Meyer.

We knelt on the floor with bowed heads. I could feel that
the room was full of people. I could smell peat. I could hear

31

a cricket chirping in the hearth. As we rose from our knees an old man ... came forward, shook hands ... handed us clay pipes ready filled with shag tobacco, and, motioning us to a wooden bench, resumed his seat ... The room was lit by three candles in brass sticks on a table which contained also a pile of clay pipes and a plate of chopped shag. In the full glow of the candlelight lay the dead woman.

H.V. MORTON
describing an Irish wake in *In Search of Ireland*, 1930

'They are all gone now, and there is nothing more the sea can do to me ... I'll have no call now to be up and crying and praying when the wind breaks from the south, making a great stir with the two noises, and they hitting one on the other. I'll have no call now to be going down and getting Holy Water in the dark nights after Samhain, and I won't

care what way the sea is when the other women will be keening.'⁵

JOHN MILLINGTON SYNGE
Riders to the Sea, 1904

'They are all together this time, and the end is come. May the Almighty God have mercy on Bartley's soul, and on Michael's soul, and on the souls of Sheamus and Patch, and Stephen and Shawn; and may He have mercy on my soul, Nora, and on the soul of every one is left living in the world.'

JOHN MILLINGTON SYNGE
Riders to the Sea, 1904

There is usually in a neighbourhood, two or three women, who are skilled beyond others in *keening*, and who make a practice of attending at wakes and funerals. These often

33

pour forth over the dead person, a lament in Irish – partly extempore, partly prepared – delivered in a kind of plaintive recitative; and at the conclusion of each verse, they lead a choral cry, in which the others who are present join, repeating throughout, 'Och, ochone!' or some such words.

> P.W. JOYCE
> *Ancient Irish Music*, 1893

> Mo ghrá thú agus mo rún!
> Tá do stácaí ar a mbonn,
> tá do bha buí á gcrú;
> is ar mo chroí atá do chumha
> ná leigheasfadh Cúige Mumhan
> ná Gaibhne Oileán na bhFionn.
> Go dtiocfaidh Art Ó Laoghaire chugham
> ní scaipfidh ar mo chumha
> atá i lár mo chroí á bhrú,
> dúnta suas go dlúth
> mar a bheadh glas a bheadh ar thrúnc
> 's go raghadh an eochair amú.
>> EIBHLÍN DUBN NÍ CHONAILL
>> from *Caoineadh Airt Uí Laoghaire*, 1773

Translation:
> You are my love and my dear one!
> Your corn stacks are standing,
> your yellow cows a-milking,
> and on my heart there's grief for you
> that Munster's province couldn't cure,
> nor the smiths of Illaunnavune,
> Till Art O Laoghaire comes to me
> my grief will not depart,
> it presses on my heart,
> shut firmly in

34

like a trunk that would be locked
and the key gone lost.
> from *The Lament for Art Ó Laoghaire*, uttered in Irish
> by his wife[6]

Perhaps there never lived a human being capable of giving the Irish cry or keene, with such exquisite effect, or of pouring into its wild notes a spirit of such irresistible pathos and sorrow. I have often been present when she 'raised the keene' over the corpse of some relative or neighbour, and my readers may judge of the melancholy charm which accompanied the expression of her sympathy, when I assure them that the general clamour of violent grief was gradually diminished, from admiration, until it became ultimately hushed, and no voice was heard but her own – wailing in sorrowful but solitary beauty …
> WILLIAM CARLETON (1794–1864)
> from fragment of autobiography; the keening woman
> was his mother

The crowd of people who assemble at … funerals sometimes amounts to a thousand, often to four or five hundred. They gather as the bearers of the hearse proceed on their way, and when they pass through any village, or when they come near any houses, they begin to cry – Oh! Oh! Oh! Oh! Agh! Agh! rising their notes from the first Oh! to the last Agh! in a kind of mournful howl. This gives notice to the inhabitants of the village that *a funeral is passing*, and immediately they flock out and follow it. In the province of Munster it is a common thing for the women to follow a funeral, to join in the universal cry with all their might and main for some time, and then to turn and ask – 'Arragh! who is it that's dead? – Who is it that we are crying for?'
> MARIA EDGEWORTH (1767–1849)
> glossary to *Castle Rackrent*

They've paid the last respects in sad tobacco
And silent is this wakehouse in its haze;
They've paid the last respects; and now their whiskey
Flings laughing words on mouths of prayer and praise.
> F.R. HIGGINS (1896–1941)
> *Pádraic Ó Conaire, Gaelic Storyteller*

No more I'll hear your sweet song, in the dewy milking
bawn,
With the kine all lowing round you, in the pale, red
light of dawn;
Some other maid will sing those songs, while you are in
the clay –
Oh! Blessed God! my heart will break for Mary of Loch
Rea.

The sun will miss the glory of your glossy, shining hair!
The youths will miss you from the dance, on summer
evenings fair!
The flowers will want your fairy step to shake their drops
away,
And I will miss your smile of love, sweet Mary of Loch
Rea.
> MICHAEL HOGAN ('The Bard of Thomond')
> 'Mary of Loch Rea'

Fond as they are of storytelling, the ballad seems to have
little attraction for our folk-people. What they delight in,
above everything else, is their love-songs; and accordingly
we find that their love-songs are not only the most
numerous but also, as a rule, by far the best intrinsically. It
is in the love-song that the folk poet shows best the beauty,

and wealth, and originality of his imagination, the depth
and tenderness of his soul.

P.H. PEARSE
from a lecture on 'The Folk Songs of Ireland', given
in January 1898

'Tis down by the lake, where the wild tree fringes its
sides,
The maid of my heart, my fair one of heaven resides;
I think as at eve she wanders its mazes along,
The birds go to sleep by the sweet wild twist of her song.

JEREMIAH JOSEPH CALLANAN (1795–1829)
'The Outlaw of Loch Lene' (translated from the Irish)

My Mary of the curling hair,
The laughing teeth and bashful air,
Our bridal morning is dawning fair,
    With blushes in the skies.
Siúil! Siúil! Siúil, a ghrá,
Siúil go socair, agus siúil, a rún,[7]
    My love! my pearl!
    My own dear girl!
My mountain maid, arise!

GERALD GRIFFIN (1803–40)
'My Mary of the Curling Hair'

O fair Una, it is you who have set astray my senses;
O Una, it is you who went close in between me and
God,
O Una, fragrant branch, twisted little curl of the
ringlets,
Was it not better for me to be without eyes than ever to
have seen you?

DOUGLAS HYDE
from a translation of the Irish song, *Úna Bhán* ('Fair
Una'), attributed to Tomás Láidir Mac Coisteala

If thou be mine, be mine both day and night,
If thou be mine, be mine in all men's sight,
If thou be mine, be mine o'er all beside –
And oh, that thou wert now my wedded bride.
    EDWARD WALSH
    translated from the Irish

The young May moon is beaming, love,
The glow-worm's lamp is gleaming, love,
How sweet to roam
Through Morna's grove,
When the drowsy world is dreaming, love!
Then awake! – the heavens look bright, my dear,
Tis never too late for delight, my dear,
And the best of all ways
To lengthen our days
Is to steal a few hours from the night, my dear!
    THOMAS MOORE
    'The Young May Moon'

The pale moon was rising above the green mountain,
The sun was declining beneath the blue sea,
When I strayed with my love to the pure crystal fountain
That stands in the beautiful vale of Tralee.
She was lovely and fair as the rose of the summer,
Yet 'twas not her beauty alone that won me –
Oh, no, 'twas the truth in her eyes ever dawning
That made me love Mary, the Rose of Tralee.
    WILLIAM P. MULCHINOCK (1820–64)
    'The Rose of Tralee'

In Dublin's fair city
Where the girls are so pretty,
I first set my eyes on sweet Molly Malone,

She wheeled her wheel-barrow
Through streets broads and narrow,
Crying 'Cockles and mussels, alive, alive oh!'
    ANON.
    old street song

Tis quite time to marry when a girl is sixteen;
Twas Willy that told me, so it's plain to be seen;
For he's handsome and manly and fit for a queen,
And just twenty years old on next Sunday,
Just twenty years old on next Sunday!
    ANON.
    old folk song, in P. W. Joyce's *Ancient Irish Music*,
    1873

Good looks are a snare that every sensible man would like
to be caught in.
    OSCAR WILDE
    The Importance of Being Earnest

Lady Bracknell: 'To speak frankly. I am not in favour of long
engagements. They give people the opportunity of finding
out each other's character before marriage, which I think is
never advisable.
    OSCAR WILDE
    The Importance of Being Earnest

You think that you are Ann's suitor; that you are the
pursuer and she the pursued; that it is your part to woo, to
persuade, to prevail, to overcome. Fool: it is you who are
pursued, the marked-down quarry, the destined prey.
    BERNARD SHAW
    Man and Superman

Woman begins by resisting a man's advances and ends by blocking his retreat.
> OSCAR WILDE
> *An Ideal Husband*

Marriage is popular because it combines the maximum of temptation with the maximum of opportunity.
> BERNARD SHAW
> *Man and Superman*

Mrs Cheveley: Their husbands. That is the one thing the modern woman never understands.
Lady Markby: And a very good thing too, dear, I dare say. It might break up many a happy home if they did.
> OSCAR WILDE
> *An Ideal Husband*

We had scarcely passed the tunnel, and entered the county of Kerry when we encountered a group that interested us greatly; on inquiry we learned that a wedding had taken place at a cottage pointed out to us, in a little glen among the mountains, and that the husband was bringing home his bride. She was mounted on a white pony, guided by as smart-looking and well dressed a youth as we have seen in the country; his face was absolutely radiant with joy; the parents of the bride and bridegroom followed; and a little girl clung to the dress of a staid and sober matron – whom we at once knew to be the mother of the bride, for her aspect was pensive – almost to sorrow; her daughter was quitting for another home the cottage in which she had been reared – to become a wife.
> MR & MRS S.C. HALL
> *Hall's Ireland*

Speak not ill of womankind,
Tis no wisdom if you do;
You that fault in woman find,
I would not be praised of you.

> EARL OF LONGFORD
> from the Irish ('Mairg a deir olc ris na mnáibh') of
> Gearóid Iarla, Earl of Desmond, late 14th century

Tradition gives depth to a man's mind. It gives him
standards to judge by, to live up to. It gives him lineage,
noblesse. It anchors him to a family, to a countryside, to a
city, to a race. He will not drift with the tide like a piece of
wreckage; he is attached to a ship that has ridden out many
a storm and will ride out many more. His race lives in him;
he thinks as they thought, their loyalties are his; his

Bringing home the bride

41

memory goes back to their beginnings; their long experience is his counsellor.

FR. DONNCHADH Ó FLOINN
Star for Irish Youth

For one armed man cannot resist a multitude, nor one army conquer countless legions; but not all the armies of all the Empires on earth can crush the spirit of one true man. And that one man will prevail.

TERENCE MAC SWINEY
Principles of Freedom

Oh! the Erne shall run red
With redundance of blood,
The earth shall rock beneath our tread,
And flames wrap hill and wood,
And gun-peal and slogan cry
Wake many a glen serene,
Ere you shall fade, ere you shall die,
My own Rosaleen!
The Judgment Hour must first be nigh
Ere you can fade, ere you can die,
My dark Rosaleen.

JAMES CLARENCE MANGAN
from the Irish. 'My Dark Rosaleen' (Mo Rósiín Dubh)
was a poetic name for Ireland

I have but a few more words to say – I am going to my cold and silent grave – my lamp of life is nearly extinguished – my race is run – the grave opens to receive me, and I sink into its bosom. I have but one request to ask at my departure from this world; it is – the charity of its silence. Let no man write my epitaph; for as no man who knows my motives dare now vindicate them; let not prejudice or ignorance asperse them. Let them and me rest in obscurity and peace; and my tomb remain uninscribed, and my memory in oblivion, until other times and other men can do justice to my character. When my country takes her place among the nations of the earth, *then* and *not till then*, let my epitaph be written.

ROBERT EMMET
from 23-year-old Emmet's *Speech from the Dock*, 19 September 1803, after he had been sentenced to death for leading a Rising for Irish freedom

And then I prayed I yet might see
Our fetters rent in twain,
And Ireland, long a province, be
A nation once again.
THOMAS DAVIS
'A Nation Once Again'

No man has a right to fix the boundary of the march of a nation; no man has right to say to his country – thus far shalt thou go and no further.

CHARLES STEWART PARNELL
speech at Cork, 21 January 1885

Was it for this the Wild Geese spread
The grey wing upon every tide;
For this that all that blood was shed,
For this Edward Fitzgerald died,
And Robert Emmet and Wolfe Tone,
All that delirium of the brave?
Romantic Ireland's dead and gone,
It's with O'Leary in the grave.
W.B. YEATS
'September 1913

We serve neither King nor Kaiser but Ireland.
> slogan on Liberty Hall, Dublin, where the Irish
> Citizen Army had its headquarters prior to Easter
> Rising, 1916

Know, that I would accounted be
True brother of that company
That sang, to sweeten Ireland's wrong,
Ballad and story, rann and song.
> W.B. YEATS
> 'To Ireland in the Coming Times'

We place the cause of the Irish Republic under the protection of the Most High God, Whose blessing we invoke upon our arms, and we pray that no one who serves that cause will dishonour it by cowardice, inhumanity, or rapine. In this supreme hour the Irish nation must, by its valour and discipline, and by the readiness of its children to sacrifice themselves for the common good, prove itself worthy of the august destiny to which it is called.
> extract from the PROCLAMATION OF THE IRISH
> REPUBLIC, Easter 1916

I assume that I am speaking to Englishmen who value their own freedom and who profess to be fighting for the freedom of Belgium and Serbia. Believe that we too love freedom and desire it. To us it is more desirable than anything in the world. If you strike us down now we shall rise again and renew the fight. You cannot conquer Ireland; you cannot extinguish the Irish passion for freedom; if our deed has not been sufficient to win freedom then our children will win it by a better deed.
> P.H. PEARSE
> Pearse, leader of the Easter Rising, speaking, 2 May
> 1916, to the courtmartial that sentenced him to
> death

'But where can we draw water,'
Said Pearse to Connolly,
'When all the wells are parched away?
O plain as plain can be
There's nothing but our own red blood
Can make a right Rose Tree.'
    W.B. YEATS
    'The Rose Tree'

Be green upon their graves, O happy Spring!
For they were young and eager who are dead!
Of all things that are young, and quivering
With eager life, be they rememberéd!
    JAMES STEPHENS
    'Spring – 1916'

I write it out in a verse –
MacDonagh and MacBride
And Connolly and Pearse
Now and in time to be,
Wherever green is worn,
Are changed, changed utterly:
A terrible beauty is born.
    W.B. YEATS
    'Easter – 1916'

This contest of ours is not on our side a rivalry of vengeance
but one of endurance – it is not they who can inflict most
but they who can suffer most will conquer.
    TERENCE MAC SWINEY
    in his speech when elected Lord Mayor of Cork,
    March 1920

On the fine summer evenings, especially on Sundays, the boys and girls collected at the cross-roads in the village (Glenosheen) to have a dance, while the old people looked on complacently, thinking of their own youthful days. Ned Goggin, our professional fiddler, supplied the music, and went home in the end with his pockets well filled with coppers. The dancing, too, was often varied by a song from some favourite singer.

> P.W. JOYCE
> *The Catholic Bulletin*, Vol. 1, 1911

Oh, the days of the Kerry dancing,
Oh, the ring of the piper's tune,
Oh, for one of those hours of gladness,
Gone, alas! like our youth, too soon!

> OLD KERRY SONG

Phelim knew all the fiddlers and pipers in the barony; was master of ceremonies at every wake and dance that occurred within several miles of him. He was a crack dancer, and never attended a dance without performing a hornpipe on a door or table. No man could shuffle, or treble, or cut, or spring or caper with him. Indeed, it was said that he could dance 'Moll Roe' upon the end of a five gallon keg, and snuff a mould candle with his heels, yet never lose the time.

> WILLIAM CARLETON
> *Phelim O Toole's Courtship and Other Stories*

My father and mother were Irish,
And I am Irish too;
I bought a wee fidil for ninepence,
And it is Irish too.
I'm up in the morning early

To greet the dawn of day,
And to the lintwhite's piping
The many's the tune I play.
    JOSEPH CAMPBELL
    The Ninepenny Fidil

On the way to market

They [the Irish] are fond of the harp, on which nearly all play, as the English do on the fiddle, the French on the lute, the Italians on the guitar, the Spaniards on the castanets, the Scotch on the bagpipe, the Swiss on the fife, the Germans on the trumpet, the Dutch on the tambourine, and the Turks on the flageolet.

> LE SIEUR DE LA BOULLAYE LE GOUZ
> translated from *Les Voyages et Observations*, Paris 1653

I had spent the preceding part of my life in my native valley (Glenosheen) in the heart of the Ballahoura mountains in Limerick, where the people were passionately fond of dancing, singing, and music of all kinds. Their pastimes, occupations and daily life were mixed up with tunes and songs. The women sang at the spinning-wheel; ploughmen whistled their melancholy plough-tunes to soothe the horses; girls sang their gentle milking songs, which the cows enjoyed,

An Irish jig

and kept quiet under their influence; parents and nurses put their children to sleep with their charming lullabies; labourers beguiled their work with songs of various kinds ... and, at the last scene of all, the friends of the dead gave vent to their sorrow in a heart-moving *keen* or lament.

    P.W. JOYCE
    The Catholic Bulletin, Vol. 1, 1911

So far from being 'lyrically derelict', the Irish language is in truth a treasure house of song, and its folk-poetry is among the most abundant of any country in Europe. The beauty of Irish music has long been universally recognised; the equal beauty of the verse to which that music was sung has been accorded no such recognition.

    DONAL O SULLIVAN
    in the Introduction to his *Songs of the Irish*, 1960

I hear men and women of Connemara singing in the fields. Sounds go a long way in this still country, I hear the click of spade against stones and a voice lifted in some old Gaelic song. I would give anything to understand it. I have never wished to understand a foreign tongue so much.

    H.V. MORTON
    In Search of Ireland, 1930

My mother, whose name was Kelly – Mary Kelly – possessed the sweetest and most exquisite of human voices ... she had a prejudice against singing the Irish airs to English words ... I remember on one occasion, when she was asked to sing the English version of that touching melody, 'The Red-haired Man's Wife', she replied, 'I will sing it for you; but the English words and the air are like a quarrelling man and wife: the Irish melts into the tune, but the English doesn't' – an impression scarcely less remarkable for its beauty than its truth. She spoke the words in Irish.

WILLIAM CARLETON (1794–1864)
from fragment of autobiography

The great game in Kerry, and indeed throughout the South is the game of 'Hurley' – a game rather rare, although not unknown in England. It is a fine manly exercise, with sufficient of danger to produce excitement; and is, indeed, par excellence, *the* game of the peasantry of Ireland. To be an expert hurler, a man must possess athletic powers of no ordinary character; he must have a quick eye, a ready hand, and a strong arm; and he must be a good runner, a skilful wrestler[8], and withal, patient as well as resolute.

MR AND MRS S.C. HALL
Hall's Ireland

... now comes the crash of mimic war, hurleys rattle against hurleys – the ball is struck and restruck ... and when some one is lucky enough to get a clear 'puck' at it, it is sent flying over the field. It is now followed by the entire party at their utmost speed ... The ball must not be taken from the ground by hand; and the tact and skill shown in taking it on the point of the hurley, and running with it half the length of the field, and when too closely pressed, striking it towards the goal, is a matter of astonishment to those who are but slightly acquainted with the play.

MR & MRS S.C. HALL
Hall's Ireland

Mackey was the laughing cavalier of the hurling fields, a man to whom every game, big or small, brought an immense amount of personal enjoyment, and an intense sense of personal challenge, a man who feared neither foe nor friend ... The more intimidating the challenge, the more eagerly did Mackey hasten to meet it, and the carefree swagger in his step as he paraded round the field in the pre-match march-past was enough to set the crowd a-tingle with the anticipation of high excitement and great deeds in store ...

> PÁDRAIG PUIRSÉAL
> describing Limerick hurler Mick Mackey in his book
> *The GAA in its Time*

For the credit of the little village!

> CHARLES J. KICKHAM
> *Knocknagow*, 1879
> the words uttered by Mat Donovan as he made his
> mighty throw to defeat the Captain in the
> sledge-throwing competition

Hurlers

The horse is the abiding passion of Ireland. There is not a trueborn Irishman, or woman, who does not turn to follow the sight of a nervous steeplechaser, high-stepping, his flanks shining with health, his hoofs ringing on the cobbles, the sweetest music to their ears.

H.V. MORTON
In Search of Ireland, 1930

Notwithstanding that the same [province of Munster] was a most rich and plentiful country, full of corn and cattle, that you would have thought they would have been able to stand long, yet ere one year and a half they were brought to such wretchedness, as that any stony heart would have rued the same. Out of every corner of the woods and glens they come creeping forth upon their hands, for their legs could not bear them; they looked like anatomies of death; they spake like ghosts crying out of their graves; they did eat of the dead carrions, happy were they if they could find them, yea, and one another soon after ... and if they found a plot of watercresses or shamrocks, there they flocked as to a feast for the time, yet not able long to continue there withal; that in short space there were none almost left, and a most populous and plentiful country suddenly made void of man and beast.[9]

EDMUND SPENSER
View of the Present State of Ireland

All the penal laws of that unparalleled code of oppression ... were manifestly the effects of national hatred and scorn towards a conquered people.

EDMUND BURKE
in a letter to Sir Hercules Langrishe, MP in *The Works of the Rt. Hon. Edmund Burke*, Vol. 111, 1845

It [the Penal Code against Irish Catholics] was a machine of wise and elaborate contrivance; and as well fitted for the oppression, impoverishment and degradation of a people, and the debasement in them, of human nature itself, as ever proceeded from the perverted ingenuity of man.

    EDMUND BURKE
    in his letter to Sir Hercules Langrishe

… here lived at the time of which we write a landlord and magistrate, named George Bond Lowe. We know little of him, except that he was thoroughly hated by the peasantry around; and his life was sought more than once. He has left amongst the people the memory of a wanton libertine and a detested tyrant; amongst the gentry, that of an intrepid and fearless magistrate. So history is written; and so it remains, and will ever remain, a rather dubious and discredited art.

    CANON P.A. SHEEHAN
    Glenanaar

Ireland is now, in one sense, in the midst, in another sense, we fear, in the beginning of a calamity, the like of which the world has never seen. Four millions of people, the majority of whom were always upon the verge of utter destitution, have been suddenly deprived of the sole article of their ordinary food.

    ISAAC BUTT
    speaking in April 1847

A plague-wind blew across the land,
Fever was in the air,
Fields were black that once were green
And death was everywhere.

    M.J. MAC MANUS
    '1849' in *Rackrent Hall and Other Poems*

Malone: 'My father died of starvation in Ireland in the Black '47. Maybe you've heard of it?'

Violet: 'The famine?'

Malone: (with smouldering passion): 'No, the starvation. When a country is full of food, and exporting it, there can be no famine.'

BERNARD SHAW

Man and Superman

There is no need to recount ... how families, when all was eaten and no hope left, took their last look at the sun, built up their cottage doors, that none might see them die nor hear their groans, and were found weeks afterwards, skeletons on their own hearth ... how starving wretches were transported for stealing vegetables by night ... and how, in every one of these years, '46, '47, and '48, Ireland

A famine funeral in the 1840s

was exporting to England food to the value of fifteen million pounds sterling, and had on her own soil at each harvest, good provision for double her own population, notwithstanding the potato blight.

JOHN MITCHEL
in the introduction to his *Jail Journal*, 1854

And they did perish; perished by hundreds, by thousands, by tens of thousands, by hundreds of thousands; perished in the houses, in the fields, by the roadside, in the ditches; perished from hunger, from cold, but most of all from famine-fever. It is an appalling picture, that which springs up to memory. Gaunt spectres move here and there, looking at one another out of hollow eyes of despair and gloom. Ghosts walk the land. Great giant figures, reduced to skeletons by hunger, shake in their clothes, which hang loose around their attenuated frames. Mothers try to still their children's cries of hunger by bringing their cold, blue lips to milkless breasts. Here and there by the wayside a corpse stares at the passers-by, as it lies against the hedge where it sought shelter.

CANON P.A. SHEEHAN
Glenanaar

The 'Wild Geese' was the name given by the romantic and sorrowful imagination of the Irish to the exiles who, like the wild birds and with their wailing cry, migrated to the continent before and after the Battle of Aughrim, and the surrender of Limerick in 1691.

STOPFORD A. BROOKE
in Preface to *With the Wild Geese* by Emily Lawless, 1902

The Irish officers and soldiers were permitted by the Treaty of Limerick to go where they pleased in ships provided by the English government. Twenty thousand sorrowing men, and Sarsfield among them, sailed to Brest and formed the bulk of the Irish Brigade in the Netherlands whose warrior-work was so far famed. They were only the forerunners of a great exodus of Irishmen flying from the iniquities of the penal laws to give their swords to France, an exodus which lasted fully a hundred years. During the heated wars of that time, from 1691 to 1745, 150,000 Irishmen are said to have died in the service of France alone. Others fought for Spain and Austria.

> STOPFORD A. BROOKE
> in the Preface to *With the Wild Geese*

The town [Cambrai] is full of Irish soldiers. They make a brave show. They are for the most part head and shoulders taller than the French, and the uniforms very fine – Clare's red coats turned back with yellow and yellow waistcoats, red vests and white breeches, and Dillon's the same but the waistcoat white, and facings are black. It is strange to see soldiers strolling in the streets and then come up with them and hear it is Irish they are talking.

> BRIDGET BOLAND
> *The Wild Geese*, 1938

When on Ramillies' bloody field,
The baffled French were forced to yield,
The victor Saxon backward reeled
Before the charge of Clare's Dragoons.

> THOMAS DAVIS
> 'Clare's Dragoons'

Soft April showers and bright May flowers
Will bring the summer back again,
But will they bring me back the hours
I spent with my brave Donal then?
Tis but a chance, for he's gone to France
To wear the fleur de lis;
But I'll follow you, my Donal dhu,
For still I'm true to you, machree. [10]
    DANNY LANE
    'On Carrigdhoun'

The illustrious and ancient house of Lacy has produced
many exalted characters. There were three branches of this
family seated at Bruree, Bruff and Ballingarry, in the county
of Limerick. The loss of their possessions did not extinguish
the memory of the achievements of their heroic ancestors.
Deprived by impolitic laws of the exercise of their inherent
military virtues, they found in the service of those

Irish militia

sovereigns, under whose banners they bled, and whose armies they often led to victory, honours as high, and distinctions as marked, as were ever conferred on any family.

JOHN FERRAR
The History of Limerick, 1787

For in far foreign fields, from Dunkirk to Belgrade,
Lie the soldiers and chiefs of the Irish Brigade.

THOMAS DAVIS
'The Battle Eve of the Brigade'

My dear Mother,
If you will sit down and calmly listen to what I say, you shall be fully resolved in every one of those many questions you have asked me. I went to Cork and converted my horse, which you prize so much higher than Fiddleback, into cash, took my passage in a ship bound for America, and at the same time paid the captain for my freight and all the other expenses of my voyage. But it so happened that the wind did not answer for three weeks; and you know, mother, that I could not command the elements. My misfortune was that when the wind served I happened to be with a party in the country, and my friend the captain never inquired after me, but set sail with as much indifference as if I had been on board …

OLIVER GOLDSMITH
from a letter to Mrs Anne Goldsmith, Ballymahon,
Co. Longford, in 'Adventure in Cork', *The Works of
Oliver Goldsmith*, 1884

'Agh! Dublin, sweet Jasus be wid you!' exclaimed a poor Irishman, as he stood on the deck of a vessel, which was carrying him out of the bay of Dublin. The pathos of this poor fellow will not probably affect delicate sensibility, because he says *wid* instead of *with*, and *Jasus* instead of *Jesus*. Adam Smith is certainly right in his theory, that the sufferings of those in exalted stations have generally most power to command our sympathy. The very same sentiment of sorrow at leaving his country, which was expressed so awkwardly by the poor Irishman, appears to every reader of taste, exquisitely pathetic from the lips of Mary, Queen of Scots – 'Farewell, France! Farewell beloved country! which I shall never more behold!'

MARIA EDGEWORTH
Essay on Irish Bulls, 1802

Irish constabulary

'There id is,' said Billy when they reached the top of the hill.

'What?'

'The cloud.'

'What cloud?'

'The cloud over Clonmel.'

'And why the cloud over Clonmel? And how did you know there was a cloud over it?'

'Because Clonmel was never wudout a cloud over id since the day Fr. Sheehy was hung,' replied Billy Hefferman.

'For what was he hung?'

'Begor, for killin' a man that was alive twenty years after,' said Billy. 'But the rale raison was because he wanted to save the people from bein' hunted, and the whole counthry turned into pasture for sheep and cattle.'

> CHARLES J. KICKHAM
> *Knocknagow*

The Irish are going with a vengeance. Soon a Celt will be as rare in Ireland as a Red Indian on the shores of Manhattan.

> THE TIMES
> the London *Times* referring to Irish post-Famine emigration

I'm bidding you a long farewell,
My Mary, kind and true!
But I'll not forget you, darling,
In the land I'm going to.
They say there's bread and work for all,
And the sun shines always there,
But I'll not forget old Ireland,
Were it fifty times as fair.

> LADY DUFFERIN
> 'Lament of the Irish Emigrant'

So adieu, my dear father, adieu, my dear mother,
Farewell to my sister, farewell to my brother;
I am bound for America, my fortune to try –
When I think on Bunclody, I'm ready to die.
    ANON.
    'The Streams of Bunclody'

Come back! Come back! Back to the land of your fathers!
Let us hear once more the sound of the soft Gaelic in our
halls; the laughter of your children beneath our roofs, the
skirl of the bagpipe and the tinkle of the harp in our courts,
the shout of our young men in the meadows by the river,
the old, heartbreaking songs from the fields, the *seanchas*[11]
here where our broken windows stare upon weed-covered
lawns. Come back! Come back! The days are dark and
short since ye went; there is no sunshine on Ireland and the
nights are long and dismal. And there in the moonlit abbey
by the river rest the bones of your kindred. Their unquiet
spirits haunt every mansion and cottage and the wail of
their Banshee[12] is over the fields and up along the hills!
They shall never rest in peace till your shadows sweep
across their tombs and your prayers, like the night winds,
stir the ivy on the crumbling walls!
    CANON P.A. SHEEHAN
    Glenanaar

I should like to have a great pool of ale for the King of
Kings;
I should like the Heavenly Host to be drinking it for all
eternity.
    ascribed to St. Brigid, 5th century, but 10th century;
    translated from the Irish by Kenneth Jackson

Some preachers will tell you that whiskey's bad,
I think so too – if there's none to be had!
> ANON.
> from *Popular Songs of Ireland*, collected by Thomas
> Crofton Croker

I sell the best brandy and sherry
To make my good customers merry,
But at times their finances
Run short as it chances,
And then I feel very sad, very.
> James Clarence Mangan's translation from the Irish
> of Seán Ó Tuama (O Tuomy), mid 18th century

O Tuomy! you boast yourself handy
At selling good ale and bright brandy
But the fact is your liquor
Makes every one sicker,
I tell you that, I, your friend Andy.
> James Clarence Mangan's translation from the Irish
> of Aindrias (Andy) MacCraith's reply to Ó Tuama's
> verse above

Then fill your glasses high,
Let's not part with lips a-dry,
Though the lark now proclaims tis dawn,
And since we can't remain,
May we shortly meet again
To fill another cruskeen lawn,[13]
Oh, to fill another cruskeen lawn.
> ANON.
> probably 18th century

I was a bould teetotaler for three long months or more,
I lived in peace and happiness, and dacent clothes I
wore;
My family was proud of me till one unlucky day
When, like a child, I was beguiled by whiskey in me tay.

Now, all ye bould teetotalers, if sober you would be,
Be careful of your company – just mind what happened
me:
Twas not the lads of Shercock nor the boys of Ballybay,
But dalin' men from Crossmaglen put whiskey in me tay.
    FR. JOHN BARTLEY
    written in the 1880s

'Poteen' is the most mysterious word in the country places
of Ireland. It is never spoken: it is always whispered. This
illicit firewater, which is distilled in the dead of night, or on
misty days which hide the smoke from the still, has always
been made in the lonely hills of Ireland.
    H.V. MORTON
    In Search of Ireland, 1930

The healthy Chestertonian approach to the bottle and glass
and little brown jug was sensible and rational and would
have been readily understood by Father Mathew. Nor was
there any reason why a man who praised the virtues of
poteen could not also praise the virtues of temperance.
    BENEDICT KIELY
    Poor Scholar, 1947

The Ulsterman is, I believe, less understood in England
even than the Southern Irishman. You frequently hear him
called an 'Ulster Scot'. Were I an Ulsterman this would
make me see red. It is so ambiguous and untrue ... If

upwards of three centuries of Irish life do not make a people
Irish what, I would like to know, does?

> H.V. MORTON
> *In Search of Ireland*, 1930

> With these folk gone, next door was tenanted
> by a wild man, an Army Officer,
> two girls, a boy, left in his quiet care,
> his wife, their mother, being some years dead.
> We shortly found that they were Catholics
> the very first I ever came to know;
> To other friends they might be Teagues or Micks;
> the lad I quickly found no sort of foe.
>
> Just my own age. His Christian Brothers School
> to me seemed cruel. As an altar boy
> he served with dread. His magazines were full
> of faces, places, named, unknown to me.
> Benburb, Wolfe Tone, Cuchulainn, Fontenoy.
> I still am grateful, Willie Morrissey.

> JOHN HEWITT
> *The Irish Dimension*

> And one read black where the other read white, his
> hope
> The other man's damnation:
> Up the Rebels, To Hell with the Pope.
> And God save – as you prefer – the King or Ireland.

> LOUIS MACNEICE
> 'Autumn Journal'

We Protestants of the Irish Republic are no longer very
interesting to anyone but ourselves. A generation ago we

were regarded dramatically as imperialistic blood-suckers, or, by our admirers, as the last champions of civilization in an abandoned island. That is the way the Roman settler may have appeared to himself and others when the legions had departed from Britain and he was left alone with the tribes he had dispossessed. Our brothers north of the border are still discussed in such colourful terms; as for ourselves, we merely exist and even that we do with increasing unobtrusiveness.

HUBERT BUTLER
Escape from the Anthill, 1985

In Ulster where you find the drumlins you will hear the drums, for the Protestant Planters usually chose the most fertile lowland areas, and I suspect that people living in such closed-in townlands tend to have a limited vision and imagination. I always like to contrast that kind of hidden landscape – Protestant landscape, shall I say? – with the open, naked bogs and hills which are naturally areas of vision and imagination, which are poetic and visionary and which represent the other tradition in Ulster.

E. ESTYN EVANS
Ulster: The Common Ground, 1984

I do not like solid blocks of opinion but, in fact, there is nothing very reassuring about our Southern Protestant incapacity for congealing into aggressive or defensive blocks. It merely means that the Ulster Protestant, a more fanatical and bitter champion of the Reformation, assumes the leadership of Irish Protestant opinion. And that leadership really belongs by tradition to the Protestants of the South, the people of Swift and Berkeley, Lord Edward Fitzgerald, Smith O'Brien, Parnell, men who often jeopardized their careers and even sacrificed their lives in the cause of an Ireland, free and united. So now our amiable inertia, our refusal to express grievances or cherish hopes about Ireland, are really delaying our ultimate unity and the reconciliation of our two diverging communities.

> HUBERT BUTLER
> *Escape from the Anthill*, 1985

It thrives through the bog, through the brake and the
mireland,
And they call it the dear little shamrock of Ireland;
The sweet little shamrock, the dear little shamrock,
The sweet little, green little, shamrock of Ireland.

> ANDREW CHERRY (1762–1812)
> 'The Dear Little Shamrock'

Every year the swallows came to our cow stalls and stables where the rafters were a maze of nests, and it was a great feather in your cap to be the one to see the first swallow and to hear the first call of the cuckoo. At night we fell asleep to the sound of the corncrake whom we thought said:

> 'Corncrake
> Out late
> Ate mate
> Friday morning.'

At that time meat was never eaten on Friday so the corncrake was breaking the fast.

> ALICE TAYLOR
> 'The Jelly Jug', in *To School through the Fields*, 1988

A fox's brush picked up fleetingly in the car headlights in a backlane after nightfall symbolises for me a dissolving way of life. But that small vixen or her cub may go on to become a predator on the edge of the hungry city. The old dialectic of the country and the city goes on in Irish life, and in

trying to sort out what it all means in a cultural context, we
are obliged to read the landscape for really telling clues.
> PATRICK J. O'CONNOR
> *Some Guides to the Irish Scene*

I will go with my father a-ploughing
To the green field by the sea,
And the rooks and the crows and the seagulls
Will come flocking after me.
I will sing to the patient horses
With the lark in the white of the air,
And my father will sing the plough-song
That blesses the cleaving share.
> JOSEPH CAMPBELL
> 'I will go with my Father A-Ploughing'

National and metropolitan needs, as these are perceived,
ensure that change is heaped upon change in and around
Dublin. A child once saw a scratching post in the form of a
cross in a field in Firhouse and exclaimed: 'That's where the
cows say their prayers!' The next day that image of bucolic
innocence was gone forever.
> PATRICK J. O'CONNOR
> *Some Guides to the Irish Scene*

There's a little singing stream in Tipperary,
And it chatters and it gurgles on its way;
Oh! I'd sit beside that stream in Tipperary
And listen to its music all the day.
> M.J. COSTELLOE

Milis an teanga an Ghaeilge.
(translation, Sweet is the Irish language.)
> SEATHRÚN CÉITINN (c. 1570–c. 1650)

The Wren Boys, who went about singing verses on
St Stephen's Day

... the words are the image of the minde, so as they proceeding from the minde must needs be affected with the words. So that the speech being Irish, the heart must needs be Irish: for out of the abundance of the heart the tongue speaketh.

> EDMUND SPENSER
> *View of the Present State of Ireland*

To grow a second tongue, as harsh a humiliation as twice to be born.

> JOHN MONTAGUE
> *A Grafted Tongue*

The first article in an Ascendancy's creed is, and always has been, that the natives are a lesser breed, and that anything that is theirs (except their land and their gold!) is therefore of little value. If they had a language and literature, it cannot have been a civilized language, cannot have been anything but a *patois* ... and as for their literature, the less said about it the better.

> DANIEL CORKERY
> in the Introduction to his *The Hidden Ireland*, 1941

The Irish language is so much spoken by the common people in the city of Cork and its neighbourhood, that an Englishman is apt to forget where he is and consider himself in a foreign city.

> EDWARD WAKEFIELD
> *An Account of Ireland, Statistical and Political*, 1812

They [the Gaelic poets of the Bardic Schools] stood firmly over the ancient ways and had but small capacity of adapting themselves to the change of times. Their existence was bound up with that of the aristocratic order which they served, and with it they fell. But their memory and their influence lived after them and, if the spoken Irish of today is perhaps the liveliest, the most concise, and the most literary in its turns of all the vernaculars of Europe, this is due in no small part to the passionate preoccupation of the poets, turning and re-turning their phrases in the darkness of their cubicles and restlessly seeking the last perfection of phrase and idiom.

    ROBIN FLOWER
    The Irish Tradition, 1947

A people without a language of its own is only half a nation. A nation should guard its language – 'tis a surer barrier, and more important frontier, than fortress or river.

    THOMAS DAVIS
    The Nation, 1 April 1843

He felt a smart of dejection that the man to whom he was speaking was a countryman of Ben Johnson. He thought:

    The language in which we are speaking is his before it is mine. How different are the words *home*, *Christ*, *ale*, *master*, on his lips and on mine! I cannot speak or write these words without unrest of spirit. His language, so familiar and so foreign, will always be for me an acquired speech. I have not made it or accepted its words. My voice holds them at bay. My soul frets in the shadow of his language.

    JAMES JOYCE
    A Portrait of the Artist as a Young Man

London was ... a haunted ruin on a hill, with the brambles over London Wall and the camp-fires of the East Angles shining in the marsh beyond the city, which they were afraid to enter; Paris was a desolation, and the sun was setting over Rome. But Armagh, the religious capital of Ireland, was the centre of European culture. During the three darkest centuries of English history Ireland was saving Greek and Latin culture for Europe.

> H.V. MORTON
> *In Search of Ireland*, 1930

Anciently, Ireland was known as *insula doctorum et sanctorum*, the island of scholars and saints. We are not concerned with the latter, but during the period of some centuries when the Gaelic civilization flourished it is probably not too much to say that the poet was primarily a scholar. He received a prolonged training in the bardic schools, and he wrote highly stylized verse in classical metres according to strict and complex rules. His poems were intended for recitation before the chieftains and nobles who were his patrons, to a harp accompaniment ...

> DONAL O'SULLIVAN
> in the introduction to his *Songs of the Irish*, 1960

The ancient traditions of the Celtic peoples, which on the Continent have been almost completely obliterated by successive invaders have, in Ireland, survived and been handed down as the particular inheritance of the nation.

> R.I. BEST
> in his Introduction to The *Irish Mythological Cycle*, by
> H. D'Arbois de Jubainville, which Best translated
> from the French, 1903

If we turn to Ireland ... we find a country where for some 1,500 years, as far back as historic knowledge can reach, one national force has overshadowed and dominated all

others. It has been the power of a great literary tradition.
ALICE STOPFORD GREEN (1847–1929)
Irish National Tradition

And before the Heroic Age the legends of the Irish Pantheon sprang mainly out of these plains between Sligo and Armagh. The wars and mischiefs of the *Tuatha Dé Danann*, the fairy hosts: the half-legends, half-histories of the Firbolgs and the Formori, and, best of all, the brilliant stories of *Cú Chulainn*, and of the Red Branch Knights – all these are of Emain Macha and of Ulster and North Connacht. So the region is for Ireland a source-place – our haunted Olympus, our Troy and our Avalon.
KATE O'BRIEN
My Ireland, 1962

The leitmotif of Gaelic society from time immemorial had been the lowing of cattle ... About these beasts centred raid and counter-raid, the ambitions of kings and queens, great battles, scandalous loves, the tremendous exploits of the sagas. In a sentence, Ireland's wealth was for centuries its soft rains, its vast pasturages, those wandering herds.
SEÁN Ó FAOLÁIN
The Irish, 1947

Now I claim for Irish literature, at its best, these excellences: a clearer than Greek vision, a more generous than Greek humanity, a deeper than Greek spirituality. And I claim that Irish literature has never lost these excellences: that they are of the essence of Irish nature and are characteristic of modern Irish folk poetry even as they are of ancient Irish epic and medieval Irish hymns.
P.H. PEARSE
from a lecture delivered December 1912

Relatively few of the impressive hero tales, which had been told in Irish, passed over into English when that language came into common use. This resulted in the loss of their 'runs' and colourful language in the new medium. Some ordinary folktales did pass through the language mesh, however, but these were but faint echoes of the former glory of Irish storytelling.

> SEÁN O' SÚILLEABHÁIN
> *Storytelling in Irish Tradition*, 1973

Poets and storytellers in homespun, humble carriers of an ancient culture, preserved until a century ago an oral tradition (*seanchas*) and an oral literature unrivalled in western Europe. Kuno Meyer, in a memorable phrase, has called the written literature of medieval Ireland 'the earliest voice from the dawn of West European civilization'.

> J.H. DELARGY
> in Sir John Rhŷs Lecture on 'The Gaelic Story-teller',
> 26 November 1945

'O Cormac, grandson of Conn,' said Carbery, 'what is the worst thing you have seen?'

'Not hard to tell,' said Cormac. 'Faces of foes in the rout of battle.'

'O Cormac, grandson of Conn,' said Carbery, 'what is the sweetest thing you have heard?'

'Not hard to tell,' said Cormac,

'The shout of triumph after victory,

Praise after wages,

A lady's invitation to her pillow.'

> ANON
> *The Instructions of King Cormac*: early 9th c.
> Translated from the Irish by Kuno Meyer.

They were the old, old tales that had come down to you ripened and sweetened like your pipe, with the ages – barring that the years of the tales were as the days of the pipe. And men and women were like little children listening even for the thousandth time, to the same tale; and could go without food or drink for fondness of hearing you tell them.

> SEUMAS MAC MANUS
> *Yourself and the Neighbours*, 1914

Éamonn Búrc, another story-teller of this parish (Carna, Connemara), gave our collector 158 tales. Some of these tales were very long; one of them runs to 34,000 words, and is one of the finest folk-tales I have ever read in any language. The story-teller died suddenly, 5 November 1942, leaving unrecorded at least as much as he had already given us (Folklore of Ireland Society). He was one of the most amazing story-tellers I have ever known.

> J.H. DELARGY
> in the Sir John Rhŷs Lecture as above

When the itch of literature comes over a man, nothing can cure it but the scratching of a pen.

> SAMUEL LOVER (1797–1868)
> *Handy Andy*

Irish poets, learn your trade,
Sing whatever is well made,
Scorn the sort now growing up
All out of shape from toe to top ...

> W.B. YEATS
> 'Under Ben Bulben'

When the times don't rhyme, then neither should poetry.
DESMOND EGAN
RTE broadcast on poetry, 1986

I hate vulgar realism in literature. The man who could call a spade a spade should be compelled to use one. It is the only thing he is fit for.
OSCAR WILDE
The Picture of Dorian Gray

It has often been observed that in their literature the insular Celts, and particularly the Irish, show a remarkable concern with the physical configuration of the land upon which they live. Every river and lake and well, every plain and hill and mountain has its own name, and each name evokes its own explanatory legend. These legends constituted a distinct branch of native tradition known as *dinnshenchas*, 'the lore of places' ... The *dinnshenchas* is thus a kind of comprehensive topography, a legendary guide to the Irish landscape.
PROINSIAS MAC CANA
Celtic Mythology

A visitor to Ireland familiar with Gaelic literature has his attention arrested everywhere in that beautiful island by many features, natural and artificial, which put him searching among his memories and clothing hill and river, rath and church and castle, with the lively and intimate colouring of long-descended tradition.
ROBIN FLOWER
The Irish Tradition

The early Irish had an extraordinary variety of personal names. Indeed, some twelve thousand names are recorded

77

in the early sources. Yet only a handful of names drawn from a rich heritage are in current use in Ireland. Thousands of them fell out of fashion at a very early period. In the later middle ages the range of names in general use was greatly narrowed, and when English became the dominant language of the country, common English, biblical and classical names frequently replaced native ones.

DONNCHADH Ó CORRÁIN and FIDELMA MAGUIRE
in Introduction to their *Gaelic Personal Names*

Ireland was one of the earliest countries to evolve a system of hereditary surnames: they came into being fairly gradually in the eleventh century, and indeed a few were formed before the year 1000 ... At first the surname was formed by prefixing Mac to the father's Christian name or O to that of a grandfather or earlier ancestor.

EDWARD MAC LYSACHT
in the Introduction to his *The Surnames of Ireland*

Away with us he's going,
The solemn-eyed:
He'll hear no more the lowing
Of the calves on the warm hillside
Or the kettle on the hob
Sing peace into his breast
Or see the brown mice bob
Round and round the oatmeal-chest
For he comes, the human child,
To the waters and the wild
With a faery, hand in hand,
From a world more full of weeping than he can understand.
W.B. YEATS
'The Stolen Child'

... the leprechaun is a very tricky little fellow, usually dressed in a green coat, red cap and knee-breeches, and silver shoe-buckles, whom you may sometimes see in the shades of evening, or by moonlight, under a bush; and he is generally making or mending a shoe: moreover, like almost all fairies, he would give the world for potheen. If you catch

him and hold him, he will, after a little threatening, show you where treasure is hid, or give you a purse in which you will always find money. But if you once take your eyes off him, he is gone in an instant; and he is very ingenious in devising tricks to induce you to look round.

  P.W. JOYCE
  Ancient Irish Music

In a shady nook one moonlight night,
A leprechaun I spied;
With scarlet cap and coat of green,
A cruiskeen by his side.
Twas tick tack tick, his hammer went
Upon a weeny shoe,
And I laughed to think of a purse of gold,
But the fairy was laughing too!

  P.W. JOYCE
  Ancient Irish Music

I have met many men and women who swear that they have heard the banshee, many of them educated people, but I have encountered only one man who claimed to have seen it. He says it was combing its hair beside a stream and stopping now and then to dip its hands in the water.

  H.V. MORTON
  In Search of Ireland

But there was a sad one among the glad fairies – the banshee – the little white woman who, in the middle of the night, on the eve of a family death, seated herself on the limb of a tree close by the home, and there, combing her long black locks, raised three heart-rending wails that sent a deadly shiver to the hearts of all within hearing, and

The Bean Chaointe (The Keening Woman)

apprised them that death was coming to claim another toll.
SEUMAS MAC MANUS
Yourself and the Neighbours

The banshee only follows families whose names begin with an 'O' or a 'Mac'.
a common saying of the Irish countryside

I was in the 'Deux Magots' in Paris one time and an American that I was introduced to asked me if I had known James Joyce. I said that I hadn't that honour, but I told him my mother had often served a meal to W.B. Yeats in Maud Gonne's house on Stephen's Green, and that the poet turned up his nose to the parsnips. 'He didn't like parsnips?' said the American reaching for his notebook. 'You're sure that is factual?'

'It is to be hoped,' I replied, 'that you're not calling my mother a liar?'

'No, no, of course not,' he said, 'but she might have been mistaken – it might have been carrots,' he added hastily.

'You must think I'm a right fool to have a mother that can't tell a carrot from a parsnip,' I said nastily.

'No, no, of course – I mean I'm sure she could but it is very important … ' He wrote in the book: *Parsnip – attitude of Yeats to.*
BRENDAN BEHAN
Brendan Behan's Island, 1962

A lifetime of happiness: No man alive could bear it: it would be hell on earth.
BERNARD SHAW
Man and Superman

To lose one parent … may be regarded as a misfortune; to lose both looks like carelessness.
OSCAR WILDE
The Importance of Being Earnest

O Rourke's noble fare
Will ne'er be forgot
By those who were there –
And those who were not!'
    DEAN SWIFT
    from the Irish of Aodh Mac Shamhráin

Robert: No eggs! No eggs! Thousand thunders, man,
            what do you mean by no eggs?
Steward: Sir, it is not my fault. It is the act of God.
Robert: Blasphemy. You tell me there are no eggs; and
            you blame your Maker for it.
Steward: Sir, what can I do? I cannot lay eggs.
    BERNARD SHAW
    Saint Joan

'Is there any news goin', Phelim?'
    'Divil a much, barrin' what you hard yourself, I suppose,
about Frank Fogarty that went mad yestherday, for risin'
the meal on the poor, and ate the ears off himself afore
anybody could see him.'
    WILLIAM CARLETON
    Phelim O Toole's Courtship and Other Stories

Brian O Linn had no breeches to wear,
He got him a sheepskin to make him a pair,
With the fleshy side out and the woolly side in,
'They are pleasant and cool,' says Brian O Linn.
Brian O Linn had no watch to wear,
He bought a fine turnip and scooped it out fair,
He slipped a live cricket under the skin,
'They'll think it is ticking,' says Brian O Linn.
    ANON.
    from the song 'Brian O' Linn'

83

I have nothing to declare except my genius.
> OSCAR WILDE
> (Wilde's reply when asked if he had anything to
> declare at the New York Custom House – quoted F.
> Harris, *Oscar Wilde*, 1918)

I was looking into an English Dictionary (yes, the other
day) and came across this mistake:

'Intelligentzia: the part of a nation (esp. the Russian)
that aspires to independent thinking.'

Now why the assumption that every nation has two
parts, one being Russian? I know that it so happens that it's
true of this country – you know that introspective crowd
from Cork ... Incidentally what sort of thinking is
dependent thinking? And look at the mess you get into if
you apply this definition to Russia itself.

A bad business, opening dictionaries; a thing I rarely do.
I try to make it a rule never to open my mouth, dictionaries
or hucksters' shops.
> FLANN O' BRIEN ('MYLES NA GOPALEEN')
> from 'Cruiskeen Lawn', *Irish Times*

Of all the books of Mr. Joyce
Ulysses is not my choice;
I think – you may not credit it –
That it should be sub-edited.
> M.J. MAC MANUS
> 'Mr James Joyce', in *So this is Dublin!*, 1927

O, look we are so! Chamber music. Could make a kind of
pun on that. It is a kind of music I often thought when she.
Accoustics that is. Tinkling. Empty vessels make most
noise. Because the accoustics, the resonance changes
according as the weight of the water is equal to the law of

84

falling water. Like those rhapsodies of Liszt's, Hungarian, gipsyeyed. Pearls. Drops. Rain. Diddle iddle addle addle oodle. Hiss. Now. Maybe now. Before.

    JAMES JOYCE
    Ulysses

Lady Bracknell: That is satisfactory. What between the duties expected of one during one's lifetime, and the duties exacted from one after one's death, land has ceased to be either a profit or a pleasure. It gives one position and prevents one from keeping it up. That's all that can be said about land.

    OSCAR WILDE
    The Importance of Being Earnest

'An' I think there's a slate,' sez she,
'Off Willie Yeats,' sez she,
'He should be at home,' sez she,
'French polishin' a pome,' sez she,
'And not writin' letters,' sez she,
'About his betters,' sez she,
'Paradin' me crimes,' sez she,
'In the *Irish Times*,' sez she ...

    PERCY FRENCH
    From *The Queen's Afterdinner Speech*
    (As overheard and cut into lengths of poetry by
    Jamesy Murphy, Deputy-Assistant-Waiter at the
    Viceregal Lodge, A.D. 1901) Note: Queen Victoria
    visited Dublin, 1901

I dislike arguments of any kind. They are always vulgar, and often convincing.

    OSCAR WILDE
    The Importance of Being Earnest

The battle raged up and down the stony field. The team we were playing was a disgusting class of team who used every kind of psychological warfare. For instance, when one of them was knocked down he rolled on the ground and bawled like a bull a-gelding.

Then there was the time when I put the ball over the goal-line and a most useful non-playing member of the opposing team kicked it back into play. We argued and there was the normal row. The referee came up and interviewed the non-playing member of the opposition, and that man replied: 'I never even saw the ball. Do you think I'd tell a lie and me at Holy Communion this morning?'

What could we say to that?

Of course we had our own methods. We never finished a game if towards the end we were a-batin'. We always found an excuse to rise a row and get the field invaded.

> PATRICK KAVANAGH
> 'Gut your Man', in *Envoy*

Young people, nowadays, imagine that money is everything, and when they grow older they know it.

> OSCAR WILDE
> *The Picture of Dorian Gray*

He gave the little Wealth he had
To build a House for fools and mad:
And shewed by one satyric Touch,
No Nation wanted it so much.

> DEAN SWIFT
> *Verses on the Death of Dr Swift*, 1731. Swift left money
> in his will for the building of St Patrick's Hospital,
> Dublin

Why should we put ourselves out of our way to do anything for posterity; for what has posterity done for us?
SIR BOYLE ROCHE

A man couldn't be in two places at once barring he was a bird.
SIR BOYLE ROCHE

The whole world is in a state of chassis.
SEÁN O CASEY
Juno and the Paycock

I can resist everything except temptation.
OSCAR WILDE
Lady Windermere's Fan

'I'd lep over the likes o' that with this little mare'

87

O woman of Three Cows, *a ghrá*, don't let your tongue thus rattle!
O, don't be saucy, don't be stiff, because you may have cattle.
I have seen – and, here's my hand to you, I only say what's true –
A many a one with twice your stock not half so proud as you.

> JAMES CLARENCE MANGAN
> 'The Woman of Three Cows (from the Irish)

The Presbyterians of the North, Gaelic by blood, have a true dash of the racial humour. A certain minister told how one of his parishioners called, late one night, sadly intoxicated, and began to put questions about a difficult point in the Calvinist doctrine of Predestination.

'See here, Donald,' said the minister; 'you're drunk, and it would suit you better to come to me with your theological questions when you're sober.'

'A knaw that, A knaw that,' said Donald, 'but ye see, when A'm sober, A don't care a damn about theology.'

> AODH DE BLÁCAM
> *Gentle Ireland*

Measaim ná fuil aon dá sheoid is luachmhaire na an Óige 's an tSláinte.

> PEIG SAYERS

Translation:
I think there are no two jewels more valuable than Youth and Health.

> *Machnamh Sean Mhná* (An Old Woman's Recollections)

Fear is more fatal than hate.

> CANON P.A. SHEEHAN

No man is rich enough to buy back his own past.
>OSCAR WILDE
>*An Ideal Husband*

The more things a man is ashamed of, the more respectable he is.
>BERNARD SHAW
>*Man and Superman*

Three slender things that best support the world: the slender stream of milk from the cow's dug into the pail; the slender blade of green corn upon the ground; the slender thread over the hand of a skilled woman.
>ANON.
>from *The Triads of Ireland*; translated from the Irish (9th century) by Kuno Meyer

My father played the melodeon,
My mother milked the cows,
And I had a prayer like a white rose pinned
On the Virgin Mary's blouse.
>PATRICK KAVANAGH
>*A Christmas Childhood*

I choose my friends for their good looks, my acquaintances for their good characters, and my enemies for their good intellects. A man cannot be too careful in the choice of his enemies.
>OSCAR WILDE
>*A Woman of No Importance*

Lord, thou art hard on mothers:
We suffer in their coming and their going.
>P.H. PEARSE
>'The Mother'

Nowadays people know the price of everything and the value of nothing.
> OSCAR WILDE
> *The Picture of Dorian Gray*

Ar a cúig a chlog ar maidin
Theastaigh an teilifís uaithi.
An féidir argóint le beainín
Dhá bhliain go leith?
> GABRIEL ROSENSTOCK
> *Teilifís*

Translation;
At five o'clock in the morning
She wanted television.
Who can argue with a little woman
Two and a half years old?
> GABRIEL FITZMAURICE

Not since Adam was a boy or Loch Gur a meadow.
> OLD SAYING

An English army led by an Irish general: that might be a match for a French army led by an Italian.
> BERNARD SHAW
> *The Man of Destiny*

The tragedy of old age is not that one is old, but that one is young.
> OSCAR WILDE
> *The Picture of Dorian Gray*

'I doubt it,' says Croker.[14]
> OLD SAYING

'A nation has apostatised,' said Father James gravely, 'when it surrenders its liberties; when it goes begging, hat in hand, for favours …'

> CANON P.A. SHEEHAN
> *The Graves at Kilmorna*

The old believe everything; the middle-aged suspect everything; the young know everything.

> OSCAR WILDE
> *Phrases and Philosophies for the Use of the Young*

Three glories of a gathering: a beautiful wife, a good horse, a swift hound.
Three things that constitute a physician: a complete cure; leaving no blemish behind; a painless examination.
Three sounds of increase: the lowing of a cow in milk; the din of a smithy; the swish of a plough.
Three candles that illume every darkness: truth, nature, Knowledge.

> ANON
> from *The Triads of Ireland*; translated from the Irish (9th century) by Kuno Keyer

Finis to all the manuscripts I've penned,
And to life's fitful fever here an end,
An end to lime-white women golden-tressed,
And in God's hand at Judgment be the rest.

> ANON. (16th century)
> Translated from the Irish by Robin Flower

Notes and Glossary

1 Albert Reynolds became Taoiseach (Head of Government) on 11 February 1992.

2 Scottia, or Scotia, was one of the names by which Ireland was known at a very early period. A large Irish colony from the north-east of Ireland crossed the narrow stretch of sea to the land then known as Alba and established there a kingdom which became known as Scotland. Abroad, at one time, an Irishman would generally be described as Scotus. For example, Johannes Scotus Eriugena, c. 810–77, who held a post at the court of the West Frankish king, Charles II, as master of the palace school, was an Irishman.

3 'Sweet Auburn' – reputed to be Lissoy, Co. Longford.

4 Glendalough – monastery founded by St Kevin, late 6th century.

5 'Keening' (from the Irish word *caoin*, 'lament') – making a ritual lament.

6 Art Ó Laoghaire (Art O Leary), a young West Cork man who had served in the Hungarian Army, was outlawed and shot dead at Carriganimmy, Co. Cork, in 1773. The famous lament for him was made by his young wife, Eibhlín Dubh (Dark-haired Eileen), of the celebrated O'Connell family of Derrynane, Co. Kerry.

7 Translation of Irish couplet:
   Come, come, come, my love,
   Come at your ease, and come, my dear.
   Approximate phonetic rendering of the Irish:
   Shule, shule, shule, a graw,
   Shule gu suckir, og-us shule, a roon.

8 Wrestling is not allowed in hurling since new rules were introduced in 1884.

9 The appalling condition to which the province of Munster had been reduced was due, in very large measure, to the scorched earth policy of the English forces in their war against the Munster Geraldines (followers of Gerald Fitzgerald, Earl of Desmond), who were in revolt against English rule 1569–83.

10 'Machree'; recte *mo chroí*, my heart, my love.

11 *Seanchas* – lore, tradition, storytelling.

12 'Banshee' – from the Irish, *bean sí*, 'woman of the fairies'. According to a widely-held belief, her wailing heralded the death of members of old Irish families, especially those whose surnames were prefixed, or entitled to be prefixed, by an O or *Mac*.

13 'Cruskeen lawn' – from the Irish, *cruíscín lán*, 'the full little jug.'

14 When John Croker, the owner of Ballinagarde House and Estate, Co. Limerick was dying, he exclaimed, 'O sweet Ballinagarde, must I leave you!' Here the storyteller takes up: 'You are going to a better place,' says his son, a minister of religion. 'I doubt it,' says Croker.

Note: There were certain deviations from standard English pronunciation in the English spoken in Ireland, especially rural Ireland, up to quite recent times. The following is a list of words, occurring in quotations in this book, which show such deviations – the deviant pronunciation is shown in brackets:

dealin'	(dalin')
decent	(dacent)
meat	(mate)
neat	(nate)
sea	(say)
tea	(tay)
treat	(thrate)
bold	(bould)